Things Change

by Ellen Bari

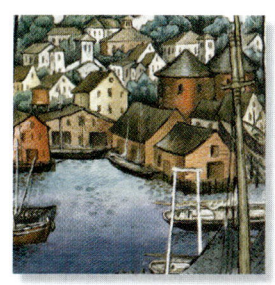

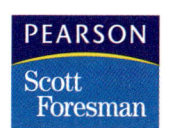

PEARSON

Scott Foresman

Editorial Offices: Glenview, Illinois • Parsippany, New Jersey • New York, New York
Sales Offices: Needham, Massachusetts • Duluth, Georgia • Glenview, Illinois
Coppell, Texas • Sacramento, California • Mesa, Arizona

Long Ago

Many homes were made of wood.
Later, **communities** changed.

Today

Some homes are made of wood or steel.
Many homes have **electricity**.

Long Ago

Many people wrote letters by hand.

Today

Many people use computers to send e-mails.

Long Ago

Many people traveled on horseback.

Today
Many people travel in cars.

Glossary

community a group of people and the place where they live

electricity a form of energy